YOGA FOR BEGINNERS

Simple techniques to boost your wellbeing

Written by Annelyse Lemmens
Translated by Emma Hanna

Health and Wellbeing 50MINUTES.com

YOGA FOR BEGINNERS

SIMPLE TECHNIQUES TO BOOST YOUR WELLBEING

- **Problem:** today, yoga is often seen as a less strenuous form of exercise that involves adopting a series of poses, some of which are more difficult than others, or as a particularly popular meditation technique. However, yoga is above all a way of boosting your physical and mental wellbeing. This guide will help you to look beyond the clichés that have grown up around yoga, gain an understanding of the discipline's underlying principles and, most importantly, learn a set of poses that you can safely practise yourself!
- **Aims:** to discover the central principles of yoga and learn some of the most basic poses, as well as the proper technique for practising them, in order to relieve stress, improve your wellbeing or even tone your physique.
- **FAQs:**
  - Do I need to be physically fit before starting to practise yoga?

- Are there precautions I should take when practising yoga?
- How often can I practise yoga?
- What are the benefits of practising yoga on a regular basis?
- How do I know if I am performing a pose correctly?
- Can yoga improve muscle definition?
- Can yoga facilitate weight loss?

No one is immune to minor ailments: headaches, moodiness, stress, insomnia, indigestion, backache and joint pain are just some of the everyday problems we all face. While it is no substitute for treatments prescribed by a qualified doctor, yoga can act in tandem with them to exponentially improve our wellbeing.

Even though yoga has been very popular in the West for several decades, many people still think of it as a strange habit – and for good reason! It is a combination of meditation and gymnastics that sometimes seems to incorporate elements of mysticism, and its practitioners (or "yogis") describe it as a holistic discipline that seeks to encourage unity of mind and body. This makes it very difficult to classify this phenomenon, which uses meditation and breathing exercises, in the form of the poses (*asanas*) the discipline is best known for, to help individuals bring their mind, body and soul into perfect harmony.

This book provides a brief overview of the history of yoga, from its origins to the many modern variants that have emerged in recent years, and explains its underlying principles and the benefits it can offer. It also features clear explanations of basic yoga poses which you can easily practise at home before working up to the world-famous "sun salutation" sequence. Plus, once you start practising yoga you will soon start getting to know yourself better and feeling fitter, more optimistic and more in tune with your emotions!

WHAT IS YOGA?

A DISCIPLINE WITH A LONG HISTORY

Although yoga is often thought of as a means of relaxation or a gentler form of exercise that focuses on self-knowledge, it is actually a much more holistic discipline which allows individuals to find (or rediscover) physical and spiritual harmony. It can therefore be considered as a kind of personal development technique that allows us to become more aware of our own senses and emotions. As such, it is hardly surprising that it is often described as a way of finding your "true self", both in a physical sense and in a mental and spiritual sense.

lated as "yoke", and in certain contexts it may also mean "method", "technique" or "discipline". It is therefore unsurprising that meditation (meaning mastery over your own thoughts), moral asceticism and control over your body are some of the key tenets of yoga!

Although Western yoga practices often emphasise the physical aspects of the discipline (through sequences of poses), yoga started out as a branch of Indian philosophy. It can be traced back to the earliest Hindu scriptures (the Vedas), which were written in Northern India in approximately 1500 BCE and were later expanded upon in epics, poems and philosophical essays (the Upanishads). However, it was not until approximately 200 BCE that these texts inspired the rise of six orthodox philosophical systems (the *darśanam*), including yoga.

After being handed down from generation to generation through oral traditions over a period of many centuries, the principles of yoga were eventually written down; according to Hindu tradition, an individual called Sage Patañjali

(c. 2nd century-4th century CE) played a particularly important role in codifying these principles in the Yoga Sutras. This "Yoga Bible" consists of 196 aphorisms (or *sutras*) which, rather than teaching readers how to strike specific poses, seeks to help them transform their inner selves. This transformation has four stages, each of which corresponds to a level of consciousness and self-control. Yoga does not have any specific religious connotations; on the contrary, it simply acts as a way for us to connect with our "inner selves". In practice, this involves engaging with our body and mind simultaneously, being aware of the present moment and acting in accordance with our needs, intentions and values. Embracing our true nature in this way also strengthens our bodies, calms our nervous system and allows us to maximise our concentration.

Yoga aims to help practitioners to overcome mental turmoil and promotes universal values such as respect for others, peace and non-violence. It is often defined according to eight major pillars: moral codes (*yama*), self-purification and study (*niyama*), poses (*asana*), breath control (*pranayama*), withdrawing of the mind from the senses (*pratyahara*), concentration (*dharana*), deep meditation (*dhyana*) and union with the object of meditation (*samadhi*). In other words, yoga is far more than just a series of poses: it is also a way for us to get to know every aspect of ourselves. Indeed, it is a truly holistic approach which allows us to strengthen both our body and mind and bring them into harmony with each other, which in turn enables us to face the challenges of modern life head-on!

A DATE FOR YOUR DIARY

In 2014, the Indian Prime Minister Narendra Modi (born in 1950), who is a practitioner of yoga himself, proclaimed 21 June of each year International Day of Yoga.

CHOOSING A SCHOOL OF YOGA: A BRIEF OVERVIEW

Given that yoga has been around for thousands of years, it should come as no surprise that many different approaches have emerged over time! While most variations of yoga are based on the same fundamental principles, many different techniques and interpretations of these principles have developed in the centuries since the philosophy first came to prominence.

Along with the five major traditional schools of yoga, dozens of "modern" approaches have also appeared in recent years. As such, you may feel more drawn to one school or another depending on your needs, expectations and comparative level of interest in spirituality, meditation and physical exercise. You may also feel drawn to the approach taught by a specific master yogi. In any case, the following overview of the main schools of yoga should help you to make a more informed decision.

QUICK TIP

Before choosing a school of yoga, take some time to ask yourself the following questions: why do you want to take up yoga? Do you want to strengthen your body, become more flexible or combat stress? Would you prefer to test your limits or just relax? Are you prepared to get to know yourself better and engage in active self-improvement?

Do you enjoy meditation and singing? The answers to these questions will give you a better idea of the approaches that would suit you best.

Traditional schools of yoga

Three of the five traditional schools of yoga have only gained a minimal foothold in the West, as they are generally considered more personal approaches to yoga and the emphasis they place on philosophy and mysticism means that they are often associated with religion. They are as follows:

- **Bhakti yoga** is primarily intended to help practitioners establish spiritual order in their lives by praying regularly, adopting an ascetic lifestyle and obeying certain Hindu teachings.
- **Jnana yoga** emphasises the importance of knowledge and understanding the universe, and seeks to identify humanity's place within it.
- **Karma yoga** focuses on the here and now. It stresses the importance of meditation, promotes conscious action and encourages

practitioners to make decisions based on their present circumstances, not future possibilities.

However, the two traditional schools of yoga which place greater emphasis on physicality have become popular worldwide:

- **Hatha yoga** focuses on poses (*asanas*). This technique is based on holding each pose for several minutes, which is considered more important than following a particular sequence. Naturally, this requires a certain degree of control over your body and breathing, as well as sustained concentration. Hatha yoga has both physical and mental benefits: it tones the body and boosts flexibility, as well as reducing stress and anxiety.
- **Ashtanga yoga**, which is also sometimes referred to as "royal yoga", was codified by the famous Sage Patañjali. It can be described as an intermediary approach, as it combines the principal characteristics of the other four major schools of yoga, although this arguably makes it the most demanding variant of yoga. In addition to control over your own body, breathing and senses, it stresses the importance of getting to know your true self, gaining

knowledge, meditation and concentration. Although it requires strict discipline, it is nevertheless one of the most accessible forms of yoga.

Modern schools of yoga

It could be said that there are as many schools of yoga as there are yogi, and changing trends, experiences and influential figures have certainly given rise to a large number of successful schools. This section provides an overview of a small selection of the most popular approaches, illustrating the incredible potential and diversity of this discipline.

- **Power yoga** is a dynamic form of yoga which is based on practising *asanas* in a heated room.
- **Shadow yoga** can be described as "meditation in motion", as it combines mental concentration and fluid movements.
- **Acroyoga** is a blend of yoga and acrobatics.
- **Laughter yoga** uses voluntary laughter as a means of promoting relaxation.
- **Iyengar yoga** is one of the many forms of yoga which are based on the teachings of a specific guru, and is named after its founder, B. K. S.

Iyengar (Indian yoga instructor, 1918-2014). This form of yoga focuses on poses and breathing exercises, and incorporates various props such as chairs, ropes and wooden blocks. This makes certain poses easier to perform, making Iyengar yoga one of the most accessible schools of yoga.

- **Sivananda yoga** emerged in the 1960s and places a great deal of importance on meditation. It typically involves focusing on relaxing and breathing rhythmically throughout a series of exercises and poses. This form of yoga is a good choice for anyone who is interested in positive thinking.
- **Satyananda yoga** is fairly similar to Sivananda yoga, and was founded by Satyananda Saraswati (Indian yoga instructor, 1923-2009). The primary aim of this approach is to adapt traditional yoga techniques to our modern way of life, and it focuses on poses and breathing exercises while also highlighting the importance of concentration and meditation in order to boost mental health and reduce anxiety.
- **Vinyasa yoga** is based on constant movement in which each pose should flow seamlessly into

the next, stressing the importance of fluidity and precision.

- **Bikram yoga** is a more controversial approach which involves following a sequence of 26 traditional yoga poses while performing a variety of breathing exercises – in a room heated to 40°C! It is a real challenge, and should only be attempted by those who are already in good physical condition.

PRINCIPLES OF YOGA

Equipment

Yoga can be practised anywhere and at any time – the only equipment you need is a yoga mat. Yoga mats are available in various colours, materials (PVC, cotton, etc.) and price ranges, though the most important element to consider is its springiness. You should also wear loose clothing which allows you to move freely and go barefoot in order to stimulate the nerve endings in your feet. It is also possible to use props such as wooden blocks, cushions and ropes to help with certain exercises if you so desire.

Meditation

Meditation is a key aspect of yoga, and Patañjali repeatedly emphasises its importance in his Yoga Sutras. Although many people believe that it is a complicated philosophical exercise, it is simply a means of cleansing your mind and soul. Given that it is not always easy to concentrate on letting your mind go blank, it is often suggested that you should start each session by repeating a "mantra" (the most famous of which is probably "om") to help you control your emotions, improve your concentration and, most importantly, clear your mind. Although some people are hesitant to try them, the use of mantras has proven highly effective.

Close your eyes for a few moments and try to detach yourself from your thoughts, letting them come and go without dwelling on them. This is not always easy, especially if you have had a busy day.

Next, try the exercise again, this time using a mantra such as "om" or simply the sound "m". Then simply concentrate on the vibration of your vocal chords and relax!

Breathing

Breathing exercises are another key element of yoga, and aim to eliminate the "blockages" between inhalation (*prana*) and exhalation (*apana*). They play a particularly important role in yoga poses which put pressure on the rib cage and when the use of certain muscles makes breathing more difficult. When performing these kinds of poses, it is very helpful to have good control over your breathing and to be able to switch between thoracic breathing and abdominal breathing.

If you are unfamiliar with the concepts of thoracic breathing and abdominal breathing, try the following exercise. Place your hands on your sides and contract your abdominal muscles. Inhale without moving them: your hands will move apart as your abdomen expands to allow the air to enter. This is thoracic breathing.

Next, use your hands to keep your sides still by pressing on them gently. In order to breathe in, you will need to relax your abdominal muscles and let your stomach expand. This is abdominal breathing.

You will need to concentrate and focus on the here and now in order to balance and adapt these two types of breathing to each yoga position. As a general rule, this balance is maintained through the constant movement of the diaphragm, which is a membrane that separates the chest from the abdomen. The best way to facilitate this movement is by trying to "stand tall" by stretching out your spine as much as possible with each of your movements.

Poses

Yoga poses, or *asanas*, are the most recognisable aspect of yoga from a Western standpoint. They can be performed quickly or slowly, be held for several minutes or form part of a fluid sequence; in any case, they should always be performed "consciously", which is why meditation and proper breathing play are such important aspects of yoga. These poses help to improve joint flexibility and strengthen musculature, particularly the so-called "deep muscles" that are closest to the bone. Poses also help to detox and massage your internal organs and, by extension, to regulate their activity. Strengthening the body in this way greatly boosts physical and mental wellbeing, as performing these movements gently often also helps us to banish certain fears, negative judgements or a lack of confidence in our own abilities.

BASIC YOGA POSES

In this section, you will discover a set of simple but essential yoga poses to get you started. In general, the philosophical principles espoused by yoga emphasise progress, not perfection, so if you are a complete novice, do not beat yourself up if your first attempts are not perfect! The important thing is to get to know your own body better and to discover your abilities and limits. Some slight discomfort is nothing to worry about, and is actually often a good sign, but yoga should never be painful – if something hurts, something is wrong and you should stop immediately.

The poses in this section are inspired by the traditional "sun salutation" and can be performed as isolated exercises, at least at first, before being combined into a proper sequence. To perform the full sequence, perform the set of suggested poses twice: first in ascending order, then in descending order.

MOUNTAIN POSE (*TADASANA*)

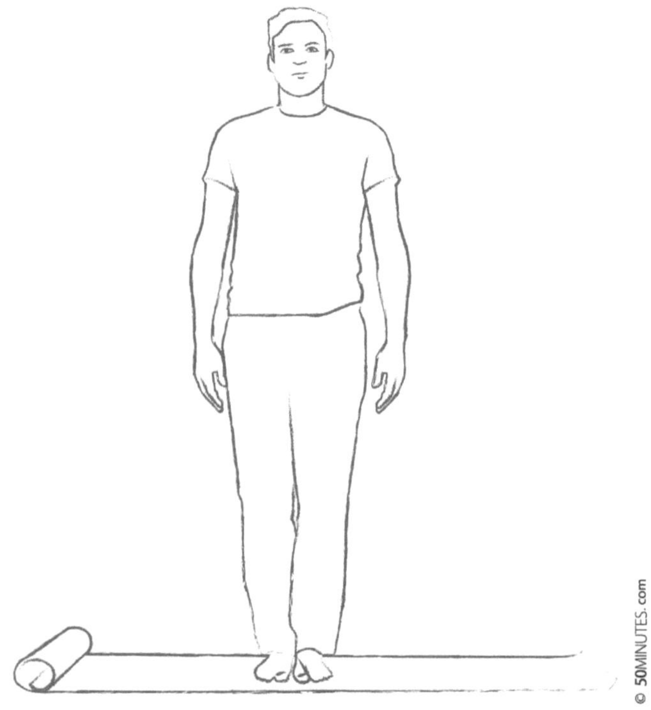

Although this pose may seem overly simple at first glance, it is a fundamental part of any yoga practitioner's repertoire.

Place your feet flat on the ground; they should be parallel and no further than shoulder-width apart. Without moving your feet, focus on your leg and abdominal muscles and gently contract them. Next, extend your spine and try to stand as tall as you can, as though a string attached to the crown of your head were pulling you upwards. Be careful: this should not straighten your back unnaturally, but rather bring its natural curves into a neutral position. Make sure to relax your shoulders and open your torso; you can leave your arms by your sides or link your hands across your chest.

QUICK TIP

In order to make sure your shoulders are properly positioned, place your hands behind you, as though in the back pockets of a pair of trousers, and let your arms relax. This will ensure that your shoulders are "open", not hunched.

If you decide to hold the pose for a few moments, you can use this opportunity to boost your concentration and feel your postural muscles at work. Keep your eyes closed and gently sway backwards and forwards, then from left to right.

Focus on the way your feet make contact with the floor and on the work done by your muscles. Now that you are in a state of "consciousness", try to stay still. It may prove more difficult than you anticipated!

This simple pose stimulates blood circulation thanks to the work done by your feet and legs, and opening your ribcage also allows you to breathe more freely. If you are feeling confident that you have mastered this *asana* and you are drawn to one of the schools of yoga that emphasises the importance of meditation, why not use this opportunity to try it out? Banish invasive thoughts and focus your attention on your own body, for example by concentrating on the following phrase: "A house built on unstable foundations cannot stand".

STANDING FORWARD BEND (*UTTANASANA*)

The Standing Forward Bend is a relatively simple pose, but it should always be performed with caution. There is a common misconception that it is simply a way of stretching the hamstrings (the muscles in the back of the thigh), like in an aerobics class, but it is actually also a means of relaxing your spine.

To enter this pose, start from a standing position such as *tadasana* and bend forward from your hips. Your back should remain straight until it forms a right angle with your legs, and you should push your buttocks backwards to help you maintain your balance. At this point, gently bend your knees (feel free to bend them more if you are not particularly flexible) and place your hands on the ground or behind your knees. Continue moving your chest downwards until your stomach comes to rest against your thighs; at this point, your shoulders should be lower than your hips. Let this weight pull you down, maintain rhythmic thoracic breathing and make sure to keep your shoulders braced, as it is essential to relax your back. If you can feel your shoulders slumping, do not hesitate to place your hands on your legs instead of the floor.

QUICK TIP

Do not use your arms as leverage to force yourself into the pose. The aim of this pose is to relax your back, and by straining yourself you risk bowing your lower back, damaging your lumbar vertebrae and giving yourself a stiff neck!

The main aim of this pose is to stretch your legs and spinal column simultaneously. It also boosts flexibility and improves blood circulation between the spinal vertebrae.

WARRIOR POSE (*VIRABHADRASANA*)

This is a somewhat more dynamic pose that will put your sense of balance to the test!

To enter this pose, stand with your feet shoulder-width apart and pointing forwards. Take a large step backward, turning your foot outwards so that it forms a right angle with your front foot. Bend your front knee to create another right angle between your shin and thigh, making sure to keep your pelvis pointing straight forwards. To help with this, the hip that corresponds to your back leg should come forward slightly, while the other should move back a little. Let your chest expand upwards and tuck in your navel. Keeping your shoulders lowered, place the palms of your hands together and slowly raise your arms above your head, watching them as they move. You should breathe freely at all times.

Did you know?

Many *asanas* are named after mythological figures; for example, the Warrior Pose is named after Virabhadra, who was one of the sons born from the hair of Shiva and was the destroyer of the arrogant. This name therefore encourages everyone who performs the pose to meditate on their humility.

This pose stretches and tones the spinal column and the muscles of the upper body; it also stretches the leg muscles, increases leg mobility and helps to improve joint flexibility over time.

PLANK POSE (*KUMBHAKASANA*)

The Plank Pose is not one of the best-known yoga poses, but it is an excellent choice for anyone hoping to tone their muscles or enhance their concentration.

To enter this pose, you can start either with your hands and feet on the floor or lying on your stomach. For the first option, extend your legs while keeping your chest and shoulders directly above your hands, with your shoulders, arms and hands forming a vertical line. If you start lying down, place your hands on either side of your shoulders and push upwards with your arms, keeping your legs extended. Your hands and feet should be firmly anchored to the floor. Contract your abdominal muscles and lower your buttocks, keeping your entire body in a straight line. Look straight ahead and breathe deeply.

> **QUICK TIP**
>
> While in the Plank Pose, you can also strengthen the muscles in your buttocks by clenching them.

You can also move from this pose into the Low Plank (*chaturanga dandasana*) by bending your arms and bringing your body closer to the ground without coming into contact with it. If you want to tone your arms (particularly your triceps), make sure to keep your elbows tucked in close to your body; however, if you are more interested in working on your pectoral muscles, let your elbows flare out.

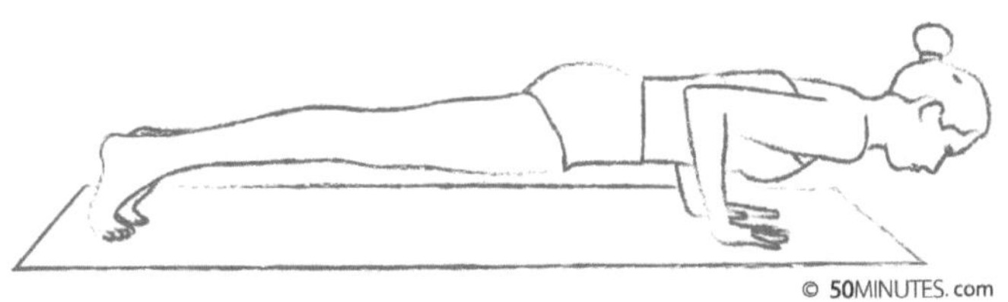

This pose allows you to stretch and tone your spine, and also strengthens the arms, shoulders, abdominal muscles, buttocks and thighs. In addition to significantly boosting muscle strength, it can also help with weight loss, energy levels and concentration.

SPHINX POSE (*ARDHA BHUJANGASANA*)

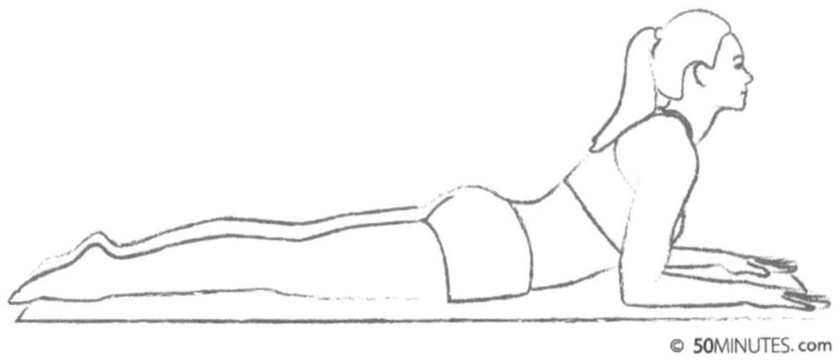

This pose, which is also known as the "Half Cobra" or "Baby Cobra" pose, is designed for relaxation and is relatively easy, although precautions should always be taken when attempting it, as is the case with any yoga pose.

To enter this pose, start by lying down on your stomach with both of your feet shoulder-width apart on the floor. Place your forehead against the ground, and then place your hands on either side of your head with the palms flat on the ground. Relax your body, and then raise your head, shoulders and chest from the floor, supporting yourself with your forearms, until your shoulders and elbows form a vertical line. Make sure to keep your head held high and relax your lower back. Look upwards, breathe slowly and concentrate on the parts of your body that are not moving, such as your pelvis, legs and feet.

QUICK TIP

To ensure that your head does not slump between your shoulders, extend your spine by gently moving your chest forward while keeping your shoulder blades pulled back.

If you feel comfortable with the Sphinx Pose, you can try moving on to the Cobra Pose (*bhujangasana*): instead of resting your weight on your forearms, support yourself with your hands, keeping the crooks of your elbows tucked in close to your body. Try to keep your pelvis as low as possible in order to keep your entire spine curved.

This pose allows you to stretch your spine quite vigorously. It also strengthens and improves the flexibility of your back and reduces pain – although performing it incorrectly can also cause pain, and anyone who suffers from lower back pain should avoid this *asana*. In any case, you should try to feel comfortable in this position. Both the Sphinx Pose and the Cobra Pose also have a stimulating effect on the body's internal organs.

DOWNWARD-FACING DOG (*ADHO MUKHA SVANASANA*)

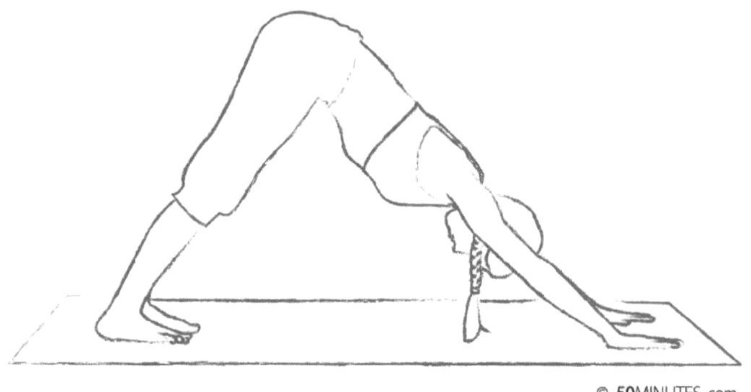

This slightly more advanced pose will help you to prepare to move into upside-down-facing positions.

To enter this pose correctly, start with your hands and feet on the ground, with your buttocks resting on your heels. Stretch your arms as far forwards as possible so that your chest is fully extended, then support yourself on your toes and extend your legs by pushing your hips upwards until your knees are no longer bent, keeping your hands anchored to the ground and your arms straight. Raise your buttocks as high as possible, press your palms into the ground and breathe steadily. Make sure to keep your back completely straight and to keep your shoulders in line with your arms. Your fingers should also be spread out to give you as much support as possible. Ideally, your heels should also be resting on the ground, but if you are not flexible enough for that then simply bend your knees a little, and do not force yourself into the pose. Your arms and legs should then be exerting equal pressure on the ground. Extend your back, place your head between your arms, and breathe from your abdomen.

QUICK TIP

Be careful not to put too much pressure on your wrists when performing this pose! If you have particularly fragile wrists, you can also support yourself on your forearms during this pose.

This pose is perfect for toning your entire body, particularly the hips and pelvis. The semi-inverted position stimulates blood flow towards the head and slows the heart rate, producing a calming effect.

HOW TO BEGIN PRACTISING YOGA REGULARLY

Have you decided to start practising yoga? Great! Remember that yoga is above all a holistic discipline, and that the benefits will only become evident over time. In order to keep your motivation up and stick with it, make sure that your yoga sessions combine both effort and relaxation.

It is important not to focus all of your attention on the physical exercises. You should also take time to meditate, as yoga is more than a form of gymnastics: it is a state of mind which is intended to improve each practitioner's emotional and mental wellbeing, as well as their physical fitness.

Make sure that you are as comfortable as possible when preparing for a session: you should wear loose clothing, have a thick mat and find a few cushions to help support you if necessary. You should also choose a suitable time to ensure that you will be able to focus on the exercises with total peace of mind: for example, try not to schedule a session directly after a meal so that you will not be doing the exercises on a full stomach. The morning is the best time to practise yoga if you are hoping to boost your concentration and increase your flexibility, but a yoga session in the evening after a busy day at work will maximise the relaxing effects. Remember that the rules of each session are up to you: if you want to open the window, turn up the air conditioning or put on some relaxing music, then feel free to do so!

While going through the poses, make sure to breathe slowly but deeply. Air should circulate freely through your lungs without any obstructions; if you find it difficult to breathe when performing a particular *asana*, you are pushing yourself too hard!

Finally, keep these three golden rules for practising yoga in mind at all times: control, moderation, regularity.

FAQS

DO I NEED TO BE PHYSICALLY FIT BEFORE TAKING UP YOGA?

In general, yoga can be practised by anyone, no matter their physique. One common misconception is the belief that it is essential to be very flexible in order to start practising yoga; on the contrary, taking up yoga can help you to become more flexible, no matter how supple you are when you start. Entering the poses correctly, respecting your limits and being aware of the possibilities available to you are all essential elements of yoga – and remember, its ultimate aim is progress, not perfection.

"I spend 10 to 20 minutes practising yoga every morning, which allows me to centre myself before starting my day. I know that yoga is a sport for some people who enjoy pushing their body to its limits, but I prefer simple stretches and meditation. But who knows, I might move towards a more physical approach someday!" (Sabrina, 34)

ARE THERE ANY PRECAUTIONS I SHOULD TAKE WHEN PRACTISING YOGA?

Anyone of any age can practise yoga, and most poses can be adapted so as not to strain a particular part of the body too much. However, if you suffer from certain conditions it may be advisable to avoid certain *asanas*; for example, individuals who experience lower back pain should not attempt the Sphinx or Cobra Poses. After all, one of the most important principles of yoga is to respect your limits.

HOW OFTEN CAN I PRACTISE YOGA?

You can practise it at any time of any day, if the mood strikes you! Given that yoga is a lifestyle, it is generally recommended to practise it on a daily basis. However, there is no point in putting yourself under excessive pressure to fulfil a daily quota, as this can often dampen your motivation. Instead, set a goal that suits your needs – for example, two or three sessions per week – and feel free to increase this frequency over time.

WHAT ARE THE BENEFITS OF PRACTISING YOGA ON A REGULAR BASIS?

Practising yoga will not necessarily yield immediate benefits. When you finish a session, you should certainly feel refreshed in a general sense, as though all the tension has been drained from your body, and over time you will learn how to pay more attention to your own body and respond to its needs more effectively. Practising yoga for one year is generally guaranteed to noticeably improve your flexibility and reduce problems with your back and joints, and in the long term it can boost your physical and psychological wellbeing.

> "I took up yoga three years ago while I was studying literature. At first I assumed it would just be a relaxing habit, but I soon noticed that I was getting more flexible. I think I even started getting physically stronger over time, and the physical exertion provided a great counterbalance to my academic studies." (Aude, 21)

HOW DO I KNOW IF I AM PERFORMING A POSE CORRECTLY?

For each pose, the main indicator of whether or not it is being performed correctly is your breathing, which should always remain even. The way you are feeling should also act as a guide: the poses are often uncomfortable, and lead you to test your limits without exceeding them, but they should never be painful.

CAN YOGA IMPROVE MUSCLE DEFINITION?

Gaining muscle is certainly never the main aim of yoga, although practising it on a regular basis generally does help to tone your entire body. Unlike other popular sports, yoga helps to develop your postural muscles, also known as "deep" muscles", which lie close to the bone. Rather than growing larger, muscles exercised during yoga tend to stretch and release tension, giving practitioners a more sculpted figure.

CAN YOGA FACILITATE WEIGHT LOSS?

Losing weight should never be your primary motivation when deciding to take up yoga. However, the mindset associated with yoga can facilitate weight loss to a certain degree, as self-awareness and paying attention to the present can boost your mental fortitude. Furthermore, improving your posture, becoming more aware of your emotions and learning to balance them can, for example, help you to cope with periods of intense stress without resorting to comfort eating. In addition, practising *asanas* allows you to sculpt your physique, drain your body of toxins and release tension. At its heart, yoga is about adopting a respectful, benevolent attitude towards yourself and the world around you, and being conscious of the implications of every choice you make and action you take. This healthier, more respectful lifestyle may in turn lead to weight loss.

We want to hear from you!
Leave a comment on your online library
and share your favourite books on social media!

FURTHER READING

BIBLIOGRAPHY

- Anderson, S. and Sovik, R. (2000) *Yoga: Mastering the Basics*. Honesdale: Himalayan Institute Press.

- Brown, C. (2008) *Quick & Easy Yoga: 5-Minute Routines for Anyone, Anytime, Anywhere*. London: Duncan Baird Publishers.

- Gasquet, B. and Bouteloup, J.-P. (2015) *Yoga sans dégâts*. Paris: Marabout.

- Kaminoff, L. and Matthews, A. (2011) *Yoga Anatomy*. Champaign: Human Kinetics.

- Patanjali. (2001) *Yoga Sutras of Patanjali*. Trans. Stiles, M. Boston: Red Wheel/Weiser.

ADDITIONAL SOURCES

- Iyengar, B. K. S. (2014) *Yoga: The Path to Holistic Health*. New York: D. K. Publishing.

IMPROVE YOUR GENERAL KNOWLEDGE

IN A BLINK OF AN EYE !

www.50minutes.com

Although the editor makes every effort to verify the accuracy of the information published, 50Minutes.com accepts no responsibility for the content of this book.

www.50minutes.com

Ebook EAN: 9782808011242

Paperback EAN: 9782808011259

Legal Deposit: D/2018/12603/307

Cover: © Primento

Digital conception by Primento, the digital partner of publishers.